S0-BIX-426

LISTENING TO NATURE

BY ABBY COLICH

BLUE OWL
BOOKS

TIPS FOR CAREGIVERS

Social and emotional learning (SEL) helps children manage emotions, learn how to feel empathy, create and achieve goals, and make good decisions. One goal of teaching SEL skills is to help children care for themselves, others, and the world around them. The more time children spend in nature and the more they learn about it, the more likely they will be to appreciate it and receive its emotional benefits.

BEFORE READING

Talk to the reader about spending time in nature.

Discuss: What sounds do you hear when you are outside? Which of those sounds are made by people? Which of those sounds come from nature?

AFTER READING

Talk to the reader about how spending time in nature makes him or her feel.

Discuss: What is your favorite sound to hear when you are outdoors? How do you feel when you listen to it?

SEL GOAL

Children may struggle with processing their emotions, and they may lack accessible tools to help them do so. Explain to children that nature can help people feel good. Nature is always available to them. Even if they can't go outside, they can look at pictures or listen to recordings of natural sounds. Encourage children to focus on the peaceful sounds of nature the next time they are struggling with their emotions. Ask them to observe how it makes them feel.

TABLE OF CONTENTS

CHAPTER 1
Noises in Nature 4

CHAPTER 2
How to Listen 8

CHAPTER 3
Ways to Listen 12

GOALS AND TOOLS
Grow with Goals 22
Mindfulness Exercise 22
Glossary 23
To Learn More 23
Index 24

CHAPTER 1

NOISES IN NATURE

Step outside. Close your eyes. What do you hear? Do cars zoom past? Maybe you hear people talking. Nature makes sounds, too. How many sounds from nature can you hear?

Birds chirp. Rain falls. Leaves rustle in the wind. Nature has many sounds. You just need to listen for them!

Spending time outside can help you be more **mindful**. Slow down and listen. Do you feel calmer? It can help you **focus**, too. You might feel happier or be able to **concentrate** better in school.

THE SCIENCE OF SOUNDS

Scientists have found that people are calmer after listening to **natural** sounds compared to **artificial** sounds.

CHAPTER 2

HOW TO LISTEN

Listening to nature is easy. Just go outside! But be sure you are prepared. Go with an adult, or have an adult's permission to be outside. Make sure you are someplace safe.

Can you hear some nature sounds where you live? You might need to travel somewhere to hear them better. Wherever you are, wear clothing that is right for the weather. If you are sitting and listening, find a comfortable spot.

You can be active and still listen to nature! Focus on all the sounds you hear. Try to figure out what is making each sound.

FOCUS ON NATURE

You may hear sounds that are not from nature. That is OK! Close your eyes. Keep your body still. Focus on the natural sounds. What do you hear? This practice could help you block out **distractions** at other times, too.

CHAPTER 3

WAYS TO LISTEN

Some sounds in nature are **soothing**. Can you hear the wind blowing? Sometimes it howls or whistles. Sometimes it seems to sigh. Your breath is like the wind. If you are feeling **anxious**, breathe in slowly. Then slowly let your breath out. Do you feel differently?

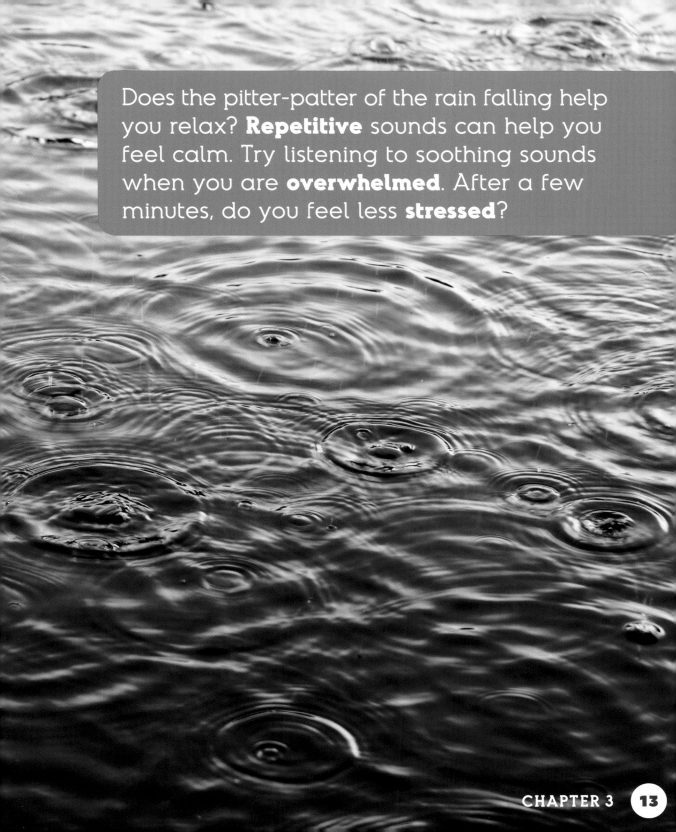

Does the pitter-patter of the rain falling help you relax? **Repetitive** sounds can help you feel calm. Try listening to soothing sounds when you are **overwhelmed**. After a few minutes, do you feel less **stressed**?

Can you think of a scary **experience** you've had? Maybe you are scared to try something new. Some sounds in nature are scary. Thunder and wind from a storm might be loud. When you are going through a scary time, remember that all storms end.

REFLECT AS YOU LISTEN

Take time to **reflect** on your thoughts as you listen. Do your thoughts change as you practice being mindful? How so?

Water moves down a river or stream. Sometimes it rushes loudly. Your thoughts can be the same way. They might be loud and distracting. Imagine your thoughts slowing down like a trickle in a stream. When you slow your thoughts, do you feel more relaxed?

If you can't go outside or can't hear any nature noises where you live, find a recording of nature sounds you like. Then put down your **device**. Close your eyes. Focus on what you hear. Notice how it makes you feel.

Remember that nature is always there. You can always use it to help you feel better. Try to listen for one sound in nature each day. Make it a **routine**. See how making nature part of your life changes how you feel.

ALL SENSES

Pay attention to your other senses, too. Do you feel the wind on your skin? What do you smell? Focusing on your senses helps you focus less on your worries and things you can't control.

GOALS AND TOOLS

GROW WITH GOALS

Nature is full of sounds. How can you make listening to nature part of your life?

Goal: Find an app of nature noises on your phone or computer. Listen to it for a few minutes before you go to bed each night. Be sure to put down your device as you relax and listen.

Goal: Listen to sounds throughout the seasons. What sounds do you hear in the spring, summer, winter, and fall? Write them down in a journal. How do they change throughout the year?

Goal: Go on a listening walk. Go with a trusted adult, or get an adult's permission. Then walk around your neighborhood. What do you hear? Which sounds are from nature? Which ones are not?

MINDFULNESS EXERCISE

Find a comfortable spot outside. Sit up straight and try to keep your body still. Close your eyes. Slowly breathe in and out. Focus on what you hear. Pick one natural sound. Focus on it for a few minutes. Then find another natural sound. Focus on that for a few minutes. After you have spent a few minutes focusing on each sound, think about how you feel. Do you feel more calm or focused?

GLOSSARY

anxious
Worried or very eager
to do something.

artificial
Not natural.

concentrate
To give all your thought
and attention to something.

device
A piece of equipment with a computer
inside, such as a smartphone or tablet.

distractions
Things that draw a person's attention
away from something.

experience
Something you do or encounter.

focus
To concentrate on something.

mindful
A mentality achieved by focusing
on the present moment and calmly
recognizing and accepting your
feelings, thoughts, and sensations.

natural
Relating to things in the world, such
as animals, plants, and the weather,
that are not made by people.

overwhelmed
Feeling completely overcome or
overpowered by thoughts or feelings.

reflect
To think carefully or seriously
about something.

repetitive
Happening again and again.

routine
A practiced sequence of actions.

soothing
Gently calming.

stressed
Experiencing mental
or emotional strain.

TO LEARN MORE

Finding more information is as easy as 1, 2, 3.

1. Go to www.factsurfer.com

2. Enter "**listeningtonature**" into the search box.

3. Choose your book to see a list of websites.

INDEX

anxious 12

birds 5

breath 12

calmer 7, 13

device 19

distractions 10, 16

focus 7, 10, 19, 20

hear 4, 9, 10, 12, 19

leaves 5

mindful 7, 15

overwhelmed 13

rain 5, 13

reflect 15

relax 13, 16

river 16

routine 20

scary 15

scientists 7

senses 20

soothing 12, 13

storm 15

stressed 13

thoughts 15, 16

weather 9

wind 5, 12, 15, 20

worries 20

Blue Owl Books are published by Jump!, 5357 Penn Avenue South, Minneapolis, MN 55419, www.jumplibrary.com

Library of Congress Cataloging-in-Publication Data

Names: Colich, Abby, author.
Title: Listening to nature / Abby Colich.
Description: Minneapolis: Jump!, Inc., 2021.
Series: Nature heals | Includes index. | Audience: Ages 7–10
Identifiers: LCCN 2020030793 (print)
LCCN 2020030794 (ebook)
ISBN 9781645278436 (hardcover)
ISBN 9781645278443 (paperback)
ISBN 9781645278450 (ebook)
Subjects: LCSH: Listening—Juvenile literature. | Mindfulness (Psychology)—Juvenile literature. | Affective education—Juvenile literature.
Classification: LCC BF323.L5 .C65 2021 (print) | LCC BF323.L5 (ebook) | DDC 155.4/18915—dc23
LC record available at https://lccn.loc.gov/2020030793
LC ebook record available at https://lccn.loc.gov/2020030794

Editor: Eliza Leahy
Designer: Michelle Sonnek

Photo Credits: EpicStockMedia/Shutterstock, cover (background); Gamut Stock Images/Alamy, cover (foreground); Daniel Doorakkers/Shutterstock, 1 (background); Jay Venkat/Shutterstock, 1 (foreground); Poring Studio/Shutterstock, 3; Spiroview Inc/Shutterstock, 4 (background); exopixel/Shutterstock, 4 (foreground); Yuriy Balagula/Shutterstock, 5; ClarkandCompany/iStock, 6–7; shapecharge/iStock, 8; all_about_people/Shutterstock, 9; Deepak Sethi/iStock, 10–11, 18–19; Wichai Prasomsri1/Shutterstock, 12; Pornanun K/Shutterstock, 13; Dark Moon Pictures/Shutterstock, 14–15; anek.soowannaphoom/Shutterstock, 16–17; Ivanova Ksenia/Shutterstock, 20–21.

Printed in the United States of America at Corporate Graphics in North Mankato, Minnesota.